POINT OF IMPACT

Revised and Updated

Heinemann Library
Chicago, Illinois

Assassination in Sarajevo

The Trigger for World War I

© 2000, 2006 Heinemann Library
a division of Reed Elsevier Inc.
Chicago, Illinois

Customer Service 888-454-2279
Visit our website at www.heinemannraintree.com

Designed by Tokay Interactive Ltd. (www.tokay.co.uk)
Printed in China by WKT Ltd

10 09 08 07 06
10 9 8 7 6 5 4 3 2 1

New edition ISBNs: 1-40349-138-0 (hardcover)
                   1-40349-147-X (paperback)

The Library of Congress has cataloged the first edition as follows:
Ross, Stewart.
       Assassination at Sarajevo : the trigger for World War One / Stewart Ross.
            p. cm. -- (Point of impact)
       Includes bibliographical references and index.
       ISBN 1-58810-074-X (library binding)
       I. World War, 1914-1918--Causes--Juvenile literature. 2. Franz Ferdinand,
Archduke of Austria, 1863-1914--Assasination--Juvenile literature. [I. Word War,
1914-1918--Causes. 2. Franz Ferdinand, Archduke of Austria,
1863-1914--Assassination.] I. Title. II. Series.

D512 .R67 2001
904.3'11--dc21
                                              00-046094

Acknowledgments
The publishers would like to thank the following for permission to reproduce photographs:
Camera Press p. **23**; Corbis (Michael St. Maur Sheil) p. **29**; Mary Evans pp. **7**, **9**, **10**, **12**, **13**, **14**, **17**, **19**, **20**, **26**; Hulton Getty pp. **4**, **5**, **8**, **16**, **21**, **25**; Imperial War Museum p. **18**; Peter Newark's Historical Pictures, pp. **24**, **27**; Peter Newark's Military Pictures, p. **15**; Popperfoto, pp. **11**, **17**, **22**.

Cover photograph reproduced with permission of Getty Images / Hulton Archive.

The publishers would like to thank Stewart Ross for his help in the preparation of this book.

Every effort has been made to contact copyright holders of any material reproduced in this book. Any omissions will be rectified in subsequent printings if notice is given to the publisher.

The paper used to print this book comes from sustainable resources.

Contents

Some words are shown in bold, **like this**. You can find out
what they mean by looking in the Glossary.

Assassination!

Two fatal shots

The scene was in Sarajevo, Bosnia, on Sunday, June 28, 1914. Beside Schiller's Café, on Franz Joseph Street, a young man gazed across the road. What should he do? His colleagues had bungled the **assassination** and the archduke had escaped. Now, the police hunt was on.

Archduke Franz Ferdinand and his wife, Sophie, smile during their visit to Sarajevo. They were shot dead shortly after this picture was taken.

Suddenly, a large, open car came around the corner, stopped, and began to reverse. It was the archduke and his party! The young assassin could not believe his luck. Without hesitating, he brought out his gun, stepped forward, and fired two shots. The first hit the archduke in the neck. The second bounced back into his wife's stomach. Both wounds were fatal. This assassination was the trigger for a war that soon involved much of the world.

What happened next?

Archduke Franz Ferdinand was heir to the throne of Austria-Hungary, a mighty European power. The government of Austria-Hungary blamed Serbia for the assassination and declared war. Although it was a small country, Serbia had a powerful friend in Russia. So, when Serbia was attacked, the Russians entered the conflict. The **allies** of Austria-Hungary and Russia were drawn in, spreading the war across Europe and beyond.

Assassinations in history

Assassination means a political murder. The word comes from the name of a group of 12th-century fanatics ("assassins") who killed their enemies as a religious duty. Throughout history, many political leaders have been assassinated. Here are some other well-known assassinations:

43 B.C.E.: Julius Caesar was stabbed to death by a group of fellow Romans.

1763: Charlotte Corday stabbed the French revolutionary leader Marat to death while he was taking a bath.

1865: John Wilkes Booth, an actor, shot dead the great U.S. president Abraham Lincoln.

1963: Lee Harvey Oswald shot dead U.S. president John F. Kennedy in Dallas, Texas.

1984: The Indian prime minister Indira Gandhi was publicly murdered by her own bodyguard.

1995: A Jewish extremist shot dead Israeli prime minister Yitzhak Rabin at a peace rally.

One small mistake...

When the United States became involved in 1917, the argument between Austria-Hungary and Serbia had grown into a terrible world war. Was anyone to blame, or was it just a series of dreadful accidents? The assassin shot Franz Ferdinand when his car took a wrong turn. Did one small mistake by the archduke's driver change the history of the world?

The shattered French town of Verdun lay on the front line between the French and German armies during World War I. Might all this devastation have resulted from two small pistol shots in Sarajevo?

To Die for Your Country

The nation state

There are over 200 **nation states** in today's world. These are countries that govern themselves. Their people mostly speak the same language and share a common culture and history. In 1914 the idea of a nation state was quite new to most people. Only in the 1860s, for example, had the separate states and cities of Italy been united into a single nation state. A similar process took place in Germany at about the same time. Serbia was also a new country. Before 1878 it had been a part of the Ottoman **Empire**.

Nationalism

The peoples of the new states and of the older ones, such as the United Kingdom and France, were passionately proud of their countries. This pride is known as nationalism. Nationalists paid great respect to their country's symbols, such as its monarch (king or queen), national anthem, and flag. Children were taught at school to love their country. Newspapers, popular songs, and poems all helped increase nationalist feelings.

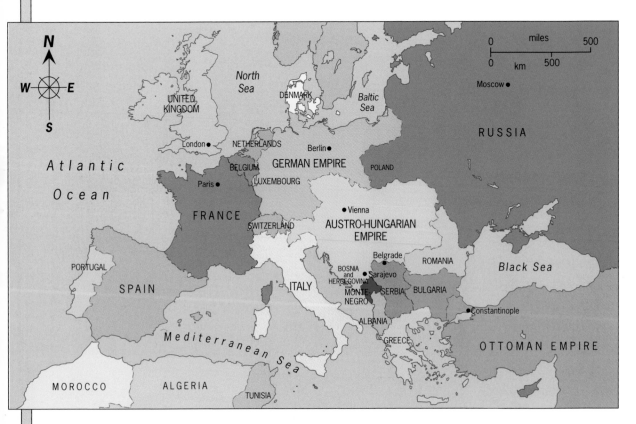

This shows Europe's divisions in 1914.

Land of Hope and Glory

A. C. Benson's famous lines in praise of Great Britain, written in 1902, are a good example of nationalist feelings common at the time:

"Land of Hope and Glory, Mother of the Free,
How shall we extol [praise] thee who are born of thee?
Wider still and wider shall thy bounds be set;
God who made thee mighty, make thee mightier yet."

Wars of independence

Nationalism helped to bind a country together, but it also had its dangers. It could lead people to believe that war was a glorious thing. Extreme nationalists said that it was noble to fight—even to die—for one's country.

Nationalism also inspired peoples who did not have their own country to fight for independence. The Serbs, for example, had been part of the Ottoman Empire since 1459. In 1876 they began a bloody war for independence. They were successful, and in 1878 the Ottomans recognized Serbia as an independent nation state.

The Serbian nation prepares to defend itself, as Serbian women undergo military training in 1908.

The Sick Man of Europe

The age of empire

In the early 20th century, much of the world was divided into empires. These consisted of several lands and peoples under the rule of one government. The British Empire was by far the largest, stretching around the globe. France, The Netherlands, Portugal, and Germany also had overseas empires. In and around Europe lay three ancient empires: the Russian Empire, the Austro-Hungarian (or Hapsburg) Empire, and the Turkish (or Ottoman) Empire.

In 1913 children at a British school celebrate Empire Day, a nationalistic holiday.

Empires were set up for several reasons. They could bring wealth and glory to the "mother country" that owned them. They were also useful markets for the mother country's goods, as well as βplaces where people from overcrowded countries could go to live. Many British people, for example, emigrated to Canada, South Africa, Australia, and New Zealand. Imperial powers (countries with empires) also took over lands to stop them from falling into the hands of other empires. This was partly why Europeans divided up Africa in the 19th century.

Imperial families

Some 19th-century empires, such as the British and the French, were governed by elected **ministers** and their administrators. Other empires, like the Russian and the Austro-Hungarian, were governed more personally. The Austro-Hungarian Empire, for instance, was also known as the Hapsburg Empire because it was ruled by Austria's **hereditary** ruling family, the Hapsburgs.

Imperialism versus nationalism

The imperial powers were eager to increase the size of their empires. This spirit of empire building is known as imperialism. Clearly, imperialism clashed head-on with nationalism, which inspired peoples to break away from imperial rule. In some regions the clash between imperialism and nationalism had serious consequences.

The sick man

In the 17th century, the Ottoman Turks had controlled a huge empire in Eastern Europe and the Middle East. Over time, however, this empire became weak and started to crumble. Its inefficient rulers failed to adopt new ideas in technology and government. By the late 19th century, the Ottoman Empire was known as the "sick man of Europe." Few people believed it would recover.

Ottoman ruler Abdul Hamid II was unable to stop his empire from being torn apart. This French cartoon of 1908 shows Bulgaria declaring itself fully independent, while Austria-Hungary seizes Bosnia and Herzegovina.

The vultures gather

Some peoples of the Ottoman Empire, such as the Greeks and Serbs, had broken away to become independent nation states. Other lands had been taken over by neighboring empires. Like jealous vultures, the imperial powers hovered over the sick man to see what else they could take.

Le Petit Journal

Le Petit Journal SUPPLÉMENT ILLUSTRÉ ABONNEMENTS

DIMANCHE 18 OCTOBRE 1908   Numéro 935

LE REVEIL DE LA QUESTION D'ORIENT
La Bulgarie proclame son indépendance. — L'Autriche prend la Bosnie et l'Herzégovine

The Powder Keg

The Balkans

The Balkans were home to a broad mix of peoples. In this mountainous region (*Balkans* comes from the Turkish word for "mountains") lived Greeks, Macedonians, Albanians, Serbs, Croats, Bosnians, Bulgarians, and Romanians. In some areas, such as Bosnia, several peoples lived alongside each other. There were also two major religions in the Balkans: Islam and Christianity. These cultural and religious differences made the region very unstable.

Imperial rivalry

The Balkans lie at the crossroads between Europe and the Middle East. Here, the frontiers of the Ottoman, Austro-Hungarian, and Russian empires met. The British also had a strong interest in the area. They did not want it to fall into the hands of a rival power. If this happened, the route through the Suez Canal to India, the jewel in the crown of the British Empire, would be threatened. In 1878 Russia and Turkey went to war. To keep Russia out of the Balkans, Britain threatened to join the war on Turkey's side, and so peace was made at the **Congress** of Berlin.

This 1912 French illustration shows how the breakup of the Ottoman Empire turned many Turkish people living in the Balkans into refugees.

Agreement for peace

Despite the Berlin agreement, by 1900 the Turks had been largely driven out of the Balkans. No imperial power had taken over from them and the region was divided into small nation states. There was much rivalry between them, causing the area to be known as the "powder keg of Europe." In 1903, worried that the situation might explode, Russia and Austria-Hungary agreed to cooperate to keep the peace there.

Fanatical hatred

"We are struck by the feelings of dislike and bitterness which Christians and Mahommedans [Muslims] feel for each other. There is no other district [than Bosnia] where the loathing between the Cross [Christianity] and the Crescent [Islam] is so strong." A report to the Austro-Hungarian government on the conditions in Bosnia, in 1875.

Conflicts in the Balkans have yet to be resolved. This 1999 picture shows the devastation caused by the troubles in Kosovo, a part of Serbia populated mostly by Albanians. Although the Serbs seized Kosovo from the Turks in 1913, the Kosovar Albanians were never happy to be part of Serbia.

Serbia's Advance

Bosnia and Herzegovina

It was agreed at the 1878 Congress of Berlin that the Austrians could look after the twin provinces of Bosnia and Herzegovina. This arrangement annoyed Serbia because a large number of Serbs lived there. Indeed, the Serbian government sometimes felt that Bosnia and Herzegovina would be better off as part of Serbia.

Aehrenthal's move

For a long time, the government of Austria-Hungary had been worried by the growth of nationalism in the Balkans. It feared that nationalism would spread into their empire and break it up. So, in 1908 the new Austro-Hungarian foreign minister, Count Lexa von Aehrenthal, decided to make a show of strength. He announced that Austria-Hungary was taking over Bosnia and Herzegovina completely and making them part of its empire.

This shows the elderly Austrian Emperor Franz Josef I (1830–1916). His government's **annexation** of Bosnia and Herzegovina in 1908 raised Serbian fears that they would be swallowed up next.

Russia's mission

Many Russians believed they had a "mission" to look after their fellow Christians in the Balkans:

"Russia's historical mission was the freeing of the Christian peoples of the Balkans from the Turkish yoke. This was almost done by the beginning of the 20th century. Nevertheless, the young Balkan countries still needed Russia's help if anyone threatened them."

Sergei Sazonov, Russia's foreign minister, in 1928.

Fury and fear

The Russians had always been close to the Serbs. They were both Slavic peoples who shared the same Orthodox Christianity. The Russians were furious, therefore, when they heard of Aehrenthal's action, but they backed away from direct confrontation. The Serbs were angry as well, and they were also frightened. Perhaps they would be next for takeover?

Russia's revenge

To show that they still had influence in the region, the Russians encouraged the Serbs to go to war (1912–13). First, the Serbs and their allies crushed the Turks. Then, they turned on Bulgaria. Their victories left Serbia bigger and stronger than ever. They also left Austria-Hungary believing that Serbia was a problem they would have to deal with sooner rather than later.

Nicholas II (1868–1918) was the last **tsar** of Russia. Weak and incompetent, he allowed Russia to be drawn into a war for which it was wholly unprepared.

Beyond the Balkans

Alliances for strength and peace

By 1914 the great European powers were divided into two groups. In 1879 Germany and Austria-Hungary had signed a Dual Alliance. This said they would help each other if they were attacked. Italy joined this alliance, making it a Triple Alliance, in 1882.

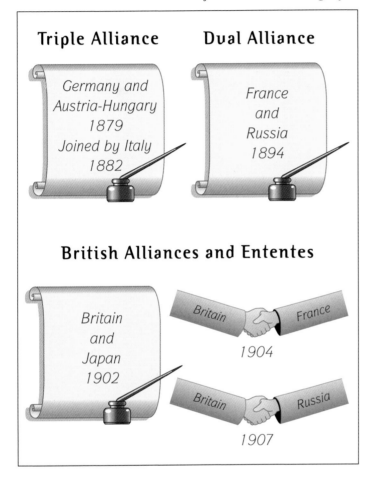

Triple Alliance

Germany and Austria-Hungary 1879 Joined by Italy 1882

Dual Alliance

France and Russia 1894

British Alliances and Ententes

Britain and Japan 1902

Britain — France 1904

Britain — Russia 1907

The Triple Alliance left France feeling isolated. So, in 1894 it formed its own Dual Alliance with Russia. For several years Britain remained outside this system of alliances, but it, too, began to feel isolated, and in 1902 it signed an alliance with Japan. This was followed, in 1904, with an **Entente Cordiale** ("friendly understanding") with France. Three years later, Britain signed a similar entente with Russia.

In the prewar years, important alliances and ententes were made. Their purpose was to keep the balance of power within Europe.

One world

These alliances and ententes were supposed to prevent war by balancing one side (the Triple Alliance) against the other (the Triple Entente). However, they also meant that events in the Balkans affected Europe and beyond. What concerned Russia, for example, also concerned her ally, France. Furthermore, because of Europe's empires, European events affected people worldwide. France's actions, for instance, affected its colonies from Indochina to North Africa.

Crisis and arms

The alliance system was tested by three serious European **crises** in the early 20th century. In 1905 and 1911, Germany challenged France's right to control Morocco. On both occasions Britain and Russia stood by France and the Germans backed down. As we have seen (page 13), in 1908 Russia backed down when Austria-Hungary took over Bosnia and Herzegovina.

After the 1911 crisis, it looked as if the alliance system was working. However, all the time the European war machine was growing—larger armies, new weapons, bigger fleets. What was all this for if not war? Would Germany or Russia be prepared to back down again?

"Expensive luxury"

Throughout the 19th century, Britain's Royal Navy ruled the seas. Then, in the 1890s, Germany began building up a powerful navy of her own. British politicians said this was unnecessary (Winston Churchill called it "an expensive luxury") and feared it would be used to attack the British Empire. In response, Britain increased the power of the Royal Navy. When Germany did the same, an expensive "naval race" began.

Britain's revolutionary new battleship, HMS *Dreadnought*, was launched in 1906. Its high speed and huge guns set in revolving turrets made all other battleships out of date. This forced the Germans to build battleships of their own, fueling the costly Anglo-German naval race.

The Visit to Bosnia

The emperor and his nephew

The Austro-Hungarian Empire was ruled by the ancient Hapsburg family. On the throne in 1914 was the narrow-minded and unsmiling Emperor Franz Josef I. He knew all about the dangers of being a public figure—his wife had been assassinated in 1898. Archduke Franz Ferdinand, the heir to the throne, was Franz Joseph's nephew. He was a cold, hard man, but he was utterly devoted to his Czech wife, Sophie.

Franz Ferdinand poses with his wife, Sophie, and their three children. Sophie, a Czech, was deeply unpopular in Austria.

The archduke's plans

Franz Ferdinand understood that many of the emperor's subjects wanted to leave the Austro-Hungarian Empire and set up their own independent states. He also knew that the Serbs living in Bosnia were among the leaders of this movement. To keep them quiet, he had plans to give them a greater say in their own government.

The Battle of Kosovo Polje

Briefly, during the 14th century, the Serbs ruled a Christian empire that covered most of the Balkans. But on June 28, 1389 (St. Vitus's Day), the invading Muslim Turks defeated them at the Battle of Kosovo Polje. Although a disaster, the heroic feats of that day have inspired Serb nationalists ever since.

Terrorist territory

In the summer of 1914, Franz Ferdinand went to Bosnia to watch the Austrian army training there. At the end of June, he planned a state visit to the important Bosnian town of Sarajevo. He wanted to impress the citizens and show that he cared about them.

The visit was brave but unwise. Sarajevo was only 50 miles (80 kilometers) from the border with Serbia, and nationalist **terrorists** were known to operate there. The date of his visit, June 28, was not well chosen, either. It was the anniversary of the Battle of Kosovo Polje, one of the most significant events in Serbian history (see page 16).

The city of Sarajevo is shown in 1893. The assassination took place just off the broad street visible to the right of the river in the top center of this picture.

Two Fatal Shots

The Black Hand

Before Franz Ferdinand's visit, Serbian terrorists had assassinated several Austro-Hungarian officials. When Danilo Ilic, the Sarajevo agent of the Black Hand terrorist group, heard of the archduke's visit, he signed up six young men and instructed them in assassination techniques. One of his recruits was Gavrilo Princip.

Bomb attack

On Sunday, June 28, Franz Ferdinand and his **entourage** arrived at Sarajevo by train. At around 10 A.M. they left for the town hall in a procession of four cars. As they passed along the Appel Quay beside the river, one of Ilic's young assassins threw a bomb at the archduke's car.

The archduke's bravery

Showing great bravery, the archduke managed to throw the bomb away before it exploded. Unfortunately, it went off beneath the car behind, injuring several people. The procession now accelerated away toward the town hall. When he arrived, Franz Ferdinand declared angrily, "So you welcome your guests here with bombs." Then, he asked to be taken to visit the injured from the earlier bomb attack.

Gavrilo Princip fired the two shots that killed the royal couple. He is shown here (far right) with two other members of the Black Hand group.

Assassination

The route to the hospital was not properly explained to the archduke's driver. He took a wrong turn into Franz Joseph Street. Having heard the news of the failed bomb attack, Gavrilo Princip had left his post and was now standing, quite by chance, outside Schiller's Café. He recognized the archduke's car at once. The moment it stopped, he advanced and fired the two fatal shots at close range. Franz Ferdinand and his wife died in the hospital fifteen minutes later.

The murder that rocked the world: this is a contemporary but rather inaccurate artist's impression of the Sarajevo assassination. Sophie was hit by a stray bullet intended for one of her husband's generals.

Gavrilo Princip

Gavrilo Princip, the nineteen-year-old son of a postman, was a member of the Young Bosnia nationalist movement and was fanatically anti-Austrian. After the assassination he took poison, but it did not work and he was arrested. Too young to be hanged, he was kept in an Austrian jail until he died of tuberculosis four years later.

The Ultimatum

Deadly evidence

Although Princip and the other terrorists were Bosnians, their weapons were Serbian. Moreover, several important Serbian officials had known about the assassination plot and done nothing to stop it. Armed with this evidence, the government of Austria-Hungary decided to end the Serbian threat once and for all.

German backing

The Austro-Hungarians did not attack Serbia right away because they were afraid Russia might come to Serbia's aid. Instead they turned to their major ally, Germany, for backing. Many in the German government believed that a European war was inevitable. They were also worried that Russia was getting stronger year by year. Therefore, deciding they had a better chance of victory if they struck first, they gave Austria-Hungary their full support.

This is a flattering image of German Kaiser Wilhelm II. He believed Germany's best hope of victory against France and Russia was to strike first—and fast.

The blank check

On July 5, 1914, the Austrian **ambassador** in Germany explained how the German kaiser promised to back Austria-Hungary against Serbia. The kaiser's eagerness was seen as a "blank check" of support: "The kaiser said ... we might in this case ... rely upon Germany's full support ... It was the kaiser's opinion that this action [against Serbia] must not be delayed."

Accept, or else...

The Austro-Hungarian government still did not go to war. Instead it sent the Serbs a ten-point **ultimatum**. This said that it would invade if the Serbs did not give Austria-Hungary complete control over their country. The Serbs had two days to reply.

War

The Serbian government accepted eight of the ultimatum's points but refused to accept Austrian officers in the Serbian army or Austrian ministers in the Serbian government. This was not good enough for Austria-Hungary, and on July 29 it declared war on Serbia.

The Russians infantry prepares for war by exercising with fixed bayonets. The enormous Russian army was seen as a "steamroller"—slow to start but unstoppable once it had got moving. The image does not show the deadly effect of machine guns.

Over by Christmas?

From Sarajevo to world war

When Serbia was attacked, Russia began to **mobilize** its forces against Austria-Hungary. In response, on August 1 Germany mobilized its forces and declared war on Russia. France, Russia's ally, began preparing for war. Eager to strike first, Germany then went to war with France. German troops moved into **neutral** Belgium, so on August 4 Britain declared war on Germany.

British troops go "over the top" during the Battle of the Somme in 1916. Ordered to walk calmly toward the enemy lines, 60,000 men were killed or wounded in the first day's attack.

Inspired by feelings of nationalism, millions on either side rushed to join the army. They believed the war would be "over by Christmas" and did not want to miss it. They were tragically mistaken. Neither side managed to get the upper hand, and other nations were drawn into the conflict. By Christmas 1915, Turkey, Italy, and Bulgaria had entered the war. The United States, threatened by German aggression, finally joined in April 1917. The European war was now the first-ever world war.

The two sides in World War 1

ALLIED POWERS	CENTRAL POWERS
France	Germany
Britain	Austria-Hungary
Russia	Ottoman Empire
Italy	Bulgaria
United States	
Serbia	
Montenegro	
Romania	
Greece	
Portugal	
Japan	
Brazil	

War of attrition

The war dragged on until November 1918. This was partly because, before the entry of the United States, the two sides were equally matched. Another reason was that defensive weapons were superior to weapons of attack. Machine guns, barbed wire, and trenches made it almost impossible for foot soldiers to attack successfully. The result was a ghastly war of **attrition**, as each side tried to wear the other down.

Total war

The war produced horror on a scale never seen before. The casualties were enormous. The hardships endured by soldiers living in cramped and unhygienic trenches were unspeakable. Moreover, the conflict affected everyone—soldiers and **civilians**. Millions were **conscripted** into the armed forces and other war work. Bombing attacks from aircraft and airships put civilians at home in direct danger. Food was **rationed** and all available industry was geared toward winning the "**total war**."

Breakthrough

At the end of 1917, Russia withdrew from the war that had caused a bloody **revolution** at home. Germany's forces could now concentrate on fighting Britain, France, and the United States. However, by then, years of war had taken their toll on all the warring nations.

In the end, Germany was defeated because it was overwhelmed. A naval blockade prevented Germany from importing food and raw materials. U.S. forces, backed by new offensive weapons—the tank and aircraft—finally gave the Allies (principally Britain, France, and the United States) sufficient power to break the stalemate and force Germany to surrender.

Italian soldiers carry a wounded comrade to safety after the Battle of Gorizia in 1916. Despite joining Germany and Austria-Hungary in the Triple Alliance in 1882, Italy entered the war on the side of the Allies in 1915.

The Lost Generation

Casualties

It is estimated that the war killed 1.8 million German soldiers and wounded a further 4.2 million. The figures for Russia were 1.7 million killed and almost 5 million wounded. For France there were 1.38 million killed and 4.2 million wounded, while for the British Empire 1 million were killed and 2.1 million were wounded.

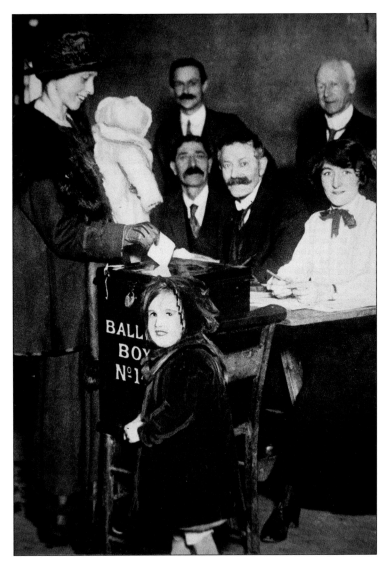

Many of those killed in the fighting were young volunteers, who represented the future of their countries. When they did not return home, their families spoke of them as the "lost generation."

Pacifism

The war was followed by an outbreak of influenza that killed as many people as the fighting. Europe was shattered and demoralized. In the late 1920s, a stream of anti-war novels and poems appeared. The most famous was Erich Remarque's novel *All Quiet on the Western Front* (1929). Some who grew up in this postwar world were **pacifists** who believed all war was wrong.

U.S. women gained the right to vote in 1920. The right to vote was seen as a kind of "reward" for the important work millions of women had done during the war.

Women prove a point

Only a few women had taken part in the fighting, but millions suffered when their countries had been invaded or through the loss of husbands, fathers, brothers, and sweethearts.

In one way, however, the war helped women. With most young men absent on the battlefield, women had successfully taken over men's jobs. This helped change attitudes toward women's rights. Between 1914 and 1939, in 28 countries worldwide women won the right to vote.

The war poets

Soldiers who openly criticized what was going on during the war risked being shot as cowards or traitors. However, some expressed their private feelings of disgust in poetry. One of these was the British officer Siegfried Sassoon.

Suicide in the Trenches

I knew a simple soldier boy
Who grinned at life in empty joy,
Slept soundly through the lonesome dark,
And whistled early with the lark.

In winter trenches, cowed and glum,
With crumps and lice and lack of rum,
He put a bullet through his brain.
No one spoke of him again.

You smug-faced crowds with kindling eye
Who cheer when soldier lads march by,
Sneak home and pray you'll never know
The hell where youth and laughter go.

Wilfred Owen was a war poet and friend of Siegfried Sassoon. Unlike Sassoon, who survived the war, Owen was killed just one week before the peace **treaty** was signed. His vivid, realistic poems, published after his death, were influential in changing people's attitude to war.

A War to End All Wars?

The empires collapse

Many governments collapsed under the strain of total war. When the fighting went against them, the European empires of Russia, Austria-Hungary, Turkey, and Germany crumbled. Britain and France were exhausted and almost **bankrupt**. In contrast, the war left the United States indisputably the wealthiest and most powerful nation on earth. As a result, the postwar world looked very different from that which had gone to war so confidently in 1914.

Revolution in Russia

The revolution early in 1917 replaced Russia's ruler, the tsar, with a Western-style government. Unwisely, it continued the war, leading to a second revolution in the fall. This brought to power the world's first **communist** government. The communists murdered the tsar and remained in power in Russia for over 70 years.

New states

The victorious Allies held a series of conferences to sort out postwar Europe. They divided the Austro-Hungarian and Ottoman empires into nation states. Austria and Hungary, for example, became separate countries. The small Balkan states, including Serbia and Bosnia, were formed into the new country of Yugoslavia.

The victors decided Germany's fate at the Versailles Conference (1919). They blamed Germany for causing the war, reduced it in size, took away its overseas colonies, and ordered it to pay $33 billion to the victors in compensation.

Tsar Nicholas II gives up his throne in 1917, having lost the respect of Russian society. His path is lined by the ghosts of Russian soldiers.

Germany's fault?

The treaty drawn up by the Versailles Peace Conference blamed Germany for starting the war. The Germans were forced to accept this blame:

"Germany and her allies accept responsibility for causing all the Allies' wartime loss and damage, which came about as a result of the war brought upon them by the aggression of Germany and her allies."

[Simplified from the Treaty of Versailles.]

The new world

The Allies announced that the war had been "the war to end all wars." They hoped to avoid future conflicts by punishing their defeated enemies and setting up the **League of Nations** to keep world peace. Neither policy worked. The League had no power to stop aggressors. Many Germans felt deeply humiliated and some dreamed of revenge. In 1933 they chose a leader who promised them that revenge: Adolf Hitler.

What was the ultimate consequence of World War I? Hitler's popularity, shown here at a 1933 rally, stemmed partly from his promise to restore German pride after the humiliation of defeat and the effects of the harsh Treaty of Versailles.

The Great Debate

What If?

Historians are interested in events, their causes, and their consequences. Asking "What if?" is not really their job. But it can sometimes help us understand why something happened. For example, might World War I never have happened if:

- Princip's shot had missed?
- The Archduke's driver had not taken a wrong turning?
- Kaiser Wilhelm II had died of cancer in 1913?

What do you think?

This map shows the countries of Europe after World War I. Were the huge changes brought about by the assassination of one man?

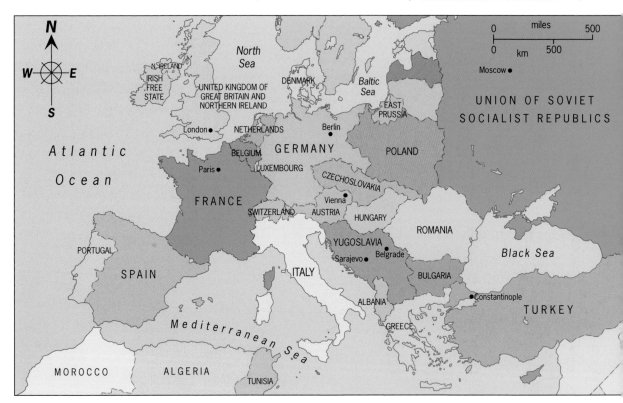

Whose Fault?

Was the Treaty of Versailles right in blaming Germany for the outbreak of World War I?

Yes!

- With its wars that led to the formation of the German Empire, Germany had created Europe's atmosphere of conflict.

- The German military buildup, its threats of force, and its aggression had all made a war more likely.

- By offering unlimited support to Austria-Hungary, the kaiser's government made an attack on Serbia almost inevitable.

- Germany declared war on Russia and France.

- Germany invaded neutral Belgium, thereby bringing Britain into the war.

No!

- All the major European powers had been preparing for war for years—they must all share the blame for what happened.

- The network of alliances and ententes made war very likely.

- No single country can be blamed for background tensions such as trade rivalry and nationalism.

- Germany was forced into war by Russia's mobilization.

- The war was started by one tiny incident—a driver's mistake—not the actions of a country.

Where do you stand?

Lest we forget: row upon row of soldiers' graves represent a wasted lives and broken dreams.

Find Out More

Using the Internet
Explore the Internet to find out more about the Sarajevo assassination and World War I. You can use a search engine, such as www.yahooligans.com or www.google.com, and type in keywords or phrases such as *Princip*, *World War I*, *trenches*, *Balkans*, or *Triple Alliance*.

More Books to Read
Allan, Tony. *20th-Century Perspectives: The Russian Revolution.*
    Chicago: Heinemann Library, 2003.

Connolly, Sean. *Witness to History: World War I.* Chicago: Heinemann Library, 2003.

Hibbert, Adam. *On the Front Line: In the Trenches of World War I.*
    Chicago: Raintree, 2006.

Ross, Stewart. *The World Wars: The Causes and Consequences of World War I.*
    Chicago: Raintree, 2003.

Timeline

1871	German Empire set up	
1879	Germany and Austria-Hungary join in a Dual Alliance	
1882	Italy forms a Triple Alliance with Germany and Austria-Hungary	
1894	France and Russia join in a Dual Alliance	
1904	Britain and France settle their differences in the *Entente Cordiale*	
1905–06	Crisis in Morocco. Germany backs down.	
1907	Britain and Russia sign an entente	
1908	Austria-Hungary takes over Bosnia and Herzegovina. Russia objects but backs down.	
1911	Second crisis in Morocco. Germany again backs down.	
1912–13	Serbia gains from two Balkan wars	
1914	**June 28**	Assassination of Archduke Franz Ferdinand
	July 5	Germany's "blank check" to Austria-Hungary
	July 23	Austria-Hungary's ultimatum to Serbia
	July 29	Austria-Hungary attacks Serbia
	July 30	Russia prepares for war
	August 1	Germany declares war on Russia
	August 3	Germany declares war on France
	August 4	British Empire declares war on Germany
	November	Turkey joins Germany and Austria-Hungary (the Central Powers)
1915	**May**	Italy joins Britain, France, and Russia (the Allies)
	October	Bulgaria joins the Central Powers
1916	**March**	Germany declares war on Portugal
	September	Bulgaria attacks Romania
1917	**April**	United States declares war on Germany
	June	Greece and Brazil join the Allies
1917	Communists come to power in Russia	
1918	**November**	Armistice ends fighting on the Western Front
1919	Treaty of Versailles between Germany and the Allies	
	League of Nations set up	
	Treaty of St. Germain ends the rule of the Hapsburgs	
	U.S. Senate rejects the Treaty of Versailles; United States backs away from European affairs	
1920	Treaty of Trianon breaks up the Austro-Hungarian Empire	
	Treaty of Sevres breaks up the Ottoman Empire	
1933	Hitler comes to power in Germany	

Glossary

ally	official friend and helper in time of trouble
ambassador	someone who represents his or her country in another country
annexation	to take possession of a country or piece of territory
assassinate, assassination	to murder, usually in public for political reasons
attrition	wearing something down steadily bit by bit
bankrupt	state of financial ruin
civilian	anyone who is not a member of the armed forces
communist	someone who believes that the state, not individual people, should own all important industry, property, and wealth
congress	international meeting
conscripted	when people are forced to join the armed forces
crisis	time of danger; the plural of *crisis* is *crises*
empire	many lands governed by one country
Entente Cordiale	friendly agreement or understanding
entourage	group of people looking after an important person
hereditary	inherited by members of the same family
League of Nations	organization established in 1919 to try to prevent war. It has since been replaced by the United Nations.
minister	member of a government
mobilize	prepare armed forces for war
nation state	country united by a single language and culture
neutral	not taking sides
pacifist	someone who believes that all use of force, particularly war, is wrong
ration	to limit food supplies in time of war or crisis and spread them out equally between people
revolution	quick, complete, and permanent change
terrorist	person who uses violence and intimidation to try to get his or her way
total war	war that involves a country's industry, agriculture, and civilian population as well as its fighting forces
treaty	written agreement between countries
tsar	emperor of Russia before 1917
ultimatum	final demand that must be obeyed to avoid punishment or retaliation

Index